LEVEL
3

Alien Ocean Animals

Rosie Colosi

NATIONAL
GEOGRAPHIC

Washington, D.C.

For Brett, who helped me dive in; for Ruby and Jane, who keep me afloat; and for Ryan, my constant lifeguard.—R.C.

Designed by YAY! Design

The author and publisher gratefully acknowledge the expert content review of this book by Maryke Musson, Curator, Two Oceans Aquarium, Cape Town, South Africa, and the literacy review of this book by Mariam Jean Dreher, professor of reading education, University of Maryland, College Park.

Author's Note
The cover shows a telescope fish, the title page features a close-up view of a pram bug, and the Table of Contents page shows a mantis shrimp.

Photo Credits
ASP=Alamy Stock Photo; GI=Getty Images; MP=Minden Pictures; NG=National Geographic Image Collection; NPL=Nature Picture Library; SCS=Science Source; SP=SeaPics.com; SS=Shutterstock

Cover, Danté Fenolio/SCS; 1, Solvin Zankl/NPL; 3, Whitcomberd/Dreamstime; 4-5, Brian J. Skerry/NG; 6, Antonio Caparo; 8-9, Paulo Oliveira/ASP; 9, Norbert Wu/MP; 10, E. Widder/HBOI/GI; 11, Solvin Zankl/NPL; 12, Jordi Chias/NPL; 13 (UP), Courtesy of NOAA/Edith A. Widder, Operation Deep Scope 2005 Exploration; 13 (LO), Courtesy of NOAA Bioluminescence and Vision on the Deep Seafloor 2015; 14, Solvin Zankl/NPL; 15, WaterFrame/ASP; 16-17, Kelvin Aitken/V&W/Image Quest Marine; 18, WaterFrame/ASP; 19-21 (ALL), David Wrobel/SP; 22, Courtesy of NOAA Office of Ocean Exploration and Research, Gulf of Mexico 2017; 23, Courtesy of NOAA Okeanos Explorer Program; 24, D. R. Schrichte/SP; 25, Bournemouth News/SS; 26 (UP), Perry Thorsvik/NG; 26 (CTR), Courtesy of Officers and Crew of NOAA Ship PISCES/Collection of Commander Jeremy Adams, NOAA Corps; 26 (LO), Humberto Ramirez/GI; 27 (UP), Courtesy of the Five Deeps Expedition; 27 (CTR), Jaffe Lab for Underwater Imaging/Scripps Oceanography/UC San Diego; 27 (LO), Luis Lamar/NG; 28, Kei Nomiyama/REX SS; 29, Solvin Zankl/NPL; 30, Danté Fenolio/GI; 31, Solvin Zankl/NPL; 32-33, randi_ang/SS; 34, Danté Fenolio/SCS; 35, Steve Downer/SCS; 35 (INSET), Flip Nicklin/MP; 36-37, Noriaki Yamamoto/MP; 38, William Chadwick, NOAA Vents Program; 39-40 (ALL), David Shale/NPL; 41, Courtesy of NOAA Okeanos Explorer Program, Galapagos Rift Expedition 2011; 42, Seatops/imageBROKER/SS; 43, Wild Horizons/UIG via GI; 44 (UP), Courtesy of Submarine Ring of Fire 2006 Exploration, NOAA Vents Program; 44 (CTR), Brian J. Skerry/NG; 44 (LO UP), Courtesy of NOAA Office of Ocean Exploration and Research, Gulf of Mexico 2017; 44 (LO LE), Solvin Zankl/NPL; 44 (LO RT), Courtesy of NOAA Office of Ocean Exploration and Research, 2016 Deepwater Exploration of the Marianas; 44 (LO LO), Danté Fenolio/SCS; 45 (UP LE), David Shale/NPL; 45 (UP RT), Gregory Ochocki/SP; 45 (LO LE), Emory Kristof/NG; 45 (LO RT), katatonia82/SS; 46 (UP), Solvin Zankl/NPL; 46 (CTR LE), randi_ang/SS; 46 (CTR RT), Antonio Caparo; 46 (LO LE), E. Widder/HBOI/GI; 46 (LO RT), Leremy/SS; 47 (UP LE), Sebastian Kaulitzki/SS; 47 (UP RT), Kei Nomiyama/REX SS; 47 (CTR LE), William Chadwick, NOAA Vents Program; 47 (CTR RT), Flip Nicklin/MP; 47 (LO LE), Norbert Wu/MP; 47 (LO RT), Danté Fenolio/GI; top border (THROUGHOUT), Elena Eskevich/SS; vocabulary box (THROUGHOUT), Maquiladora/SS

Library of Congress Cataloging-in-Publication Data

Names: Colosi, Rosie, author. | National Geographic Society (U.S.)
Title: Alien ocean animals / by Rosie Colosi.
Description: Washington, DC : National Geographic Kids, [2020] | Series: National Geographic readers | Audience: Age 4-6. | Audience: K to Grade 3. | Identifiers: LCCN 2019007817 (print) | LCCN 2019008448 (ebook) | ISBN 9781426337079 (e-book) | ISBN 9781426337086 (e-book) | ISBN 9781426337055 (paperback) | ISBN 9781426337062 (hardcover)
Subjects: LCSH: Marine animals--Juvenile literature. | Deep-sea animals--Juvenile literature.
Classification: LCC QL122.2 (ebook) | LCC QL122.2 .C6526 2020 (print) | DDC 591.77--dc23
LC record available at https://lccn.loc.gov/2019007817

National Geographic supports K–12 educators with ELA Common Core Resources. Visit natgeoed.org/commoncore for more information.

Printed in the United States of America
19/WOR/1

Table of Contents

Out of This World ... 4

Enter the Midnight Zone ... 6

Light in the Darkness ... 8

Open Wide! ... 14

Staying Safe ... 20

6 Cool Facts About Ocean Exploration ... 26

Hidden Away ... 28

Eyes of the Deep ... 32

Underwater Party Animals ... 38

A Lot More to Explore! ... 42

Quiz Whiz ... 44

Glossary ... 46

Index ... 48

Out of This World

The deepest parts of the ocean are some of the last places on Earth left to explore. It's hard for scientists to travel there. It's nearly freezing and almost completely dark.

Animals that live there look different from animals in other parts of the ocean. You might even say they look like aliens from outer space. Let's dive in and meet some of these alien ocean animals!

This submersible, called *DeepSee*, explores the ocean floor near Cocos Island, Costa Rica.

Enter the Midnight Zone

The ocean is divided into three main areas.

SUNLIGHT ZONE
Depth: Sea level to 656 feet
People usually fish and swim here.

TWILIGHT ZONE
Depth: 657 feet to 3,280 feet
Only a small amount of light filters through, and the water gets colder.

MIDNIGHT ZONE
Depth: Below 3,280 feet
Temperatures can be close to freezing and it's almost completely dark in this zone. Since there is no sunlight, plants can't grow here.

weird but true!

An area called Challenger Deep in the Pacific Ocean is the deepest place on Earth. At 36,070 feet deep, it's deeper than Mount Everest is tall!

The Midnight Zone is the largest habitat on Earth, but it's a hard place to live. An ocean creature living there has thousands of feet of water above it. All of that water presses down, causing anything floating there to feel a lot of pressure.

The deeper an animal swims, the more pressure it feels. Few animals can survive this high pressure. Since no plants and few animals live there, not much food is available for animals that live in the Midnight Zone.

Water Words

HABITAT: A place where animals or plants naturally live

PRESSURE: The force pushing on something

Light in the Darkness

Sunlight doesn't reach the Midnight Zone. But it's not completely dark. There's still some light—it's light that the animals make themselves!

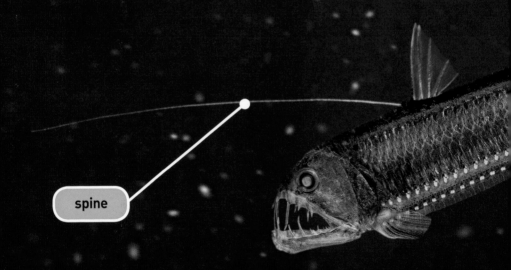

spine

The Sloane's viperfish is one of the fiercest animals in the deep sea.

This viperfish has a long spine with a tiny light patch at the tip. The light dangles above its head and flashes on and off. Prey swims closer to see if the light is food. Then the viperfish bites the prey with its sharp teeth.

Many predators have light that attracts prey. But the smalltooth dragonfish has a special red light that most fish can't see. The patches of red light under its eyes help the dragonfish find prey in the dark water. But prey can't see the dragonfish coming!

Water Word

PREDATOR: An animal that hunts and eats other animals

The long arms on this squid easily reach out and grab prey.

The Atlantic long-arm squid has rows of light patches on its long arms. The light patches make the squid's prey think it's a jellyfish. The prey thinks a jellyfish won't harm it. So when the prey swims close enough, the squid can grab the animal and eat it.

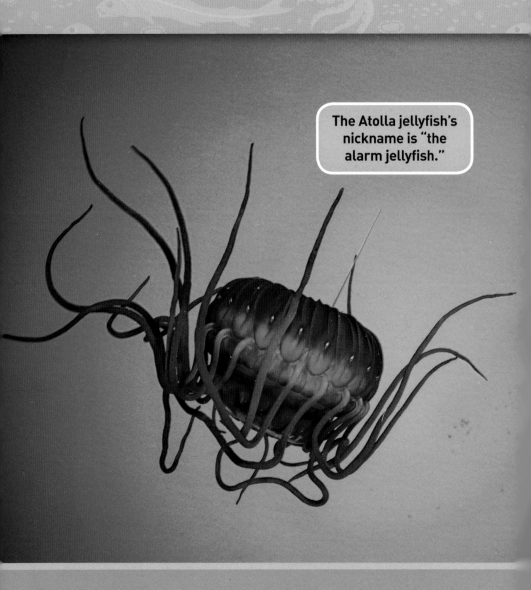

The Atolla jellyfish's nickname is "the alarm jellyfish."

The Atolla jellyfish uses light as an alarm. If a predator tries to attack this jellyfish, the jellyfish "screams" by flashing blue lights around its middle. The lights spin like the ones on top of a police car.

The lights attract the attention of other, bigger predators. The bigger predators attack the smaller predator. Then the jellyfish has a chance to swim away.

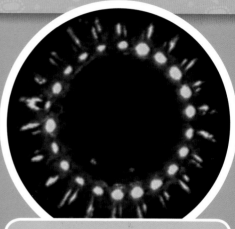

The lights of the Atolla jellyfish are blue. Blue light travels the greatest distance underwater.

Alarming Attraction

The Atolla jellyfish alarm system works so well that scientists used the idea to create electronic jellyfish (or e-jellies). An e-jelly has the same flashing lights as the Atolla jellyfish. It also has a camera to record animals that swim by. Scientists hope to study large predators, like cutthroat eels, that the e-jelly's lights attract.

Open Wide!

Animals in the Midnight Zone have adaptations that help them live there. In the deep ocean, there isn't much to eat. So, many animals there have special mouths to help them hunt and survive.

The hairy frogfish can swallow prey as big as its own body. When it spots prey, the frogfish stretches its mouth up to 12 times wider than normal. *Gulp!* The fish swallows the prey whole. Then the frogfish closes its throat so dinner can't escape!

Hairy frogfish aren't hairy! Their "hairs" are actually small spines that cover their bodies.

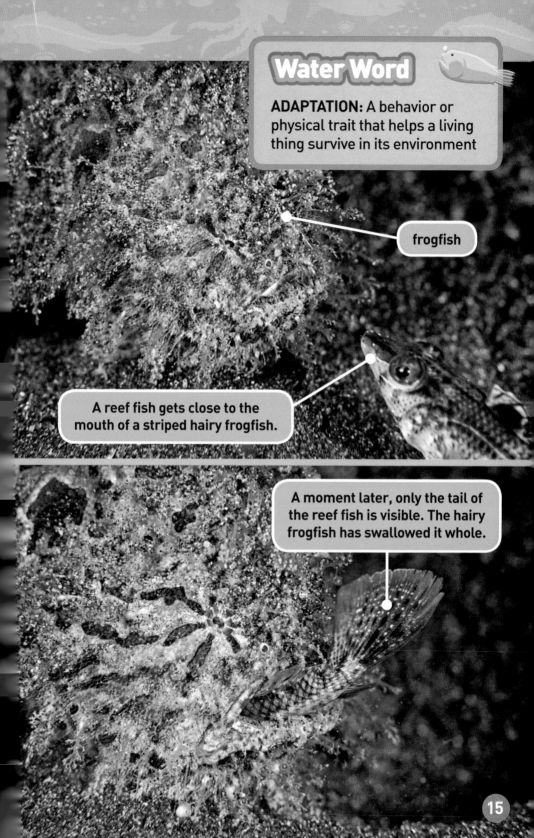

frogfish

A reef fish gets close to the mouth of a striped hairy frogfish.

A moment later, only the tail of the reef fish is visible. The hairy frogfish has swallowed it whole.

15

It's hard to find and catch food in the Midnight Zone. So animals must hang on to their food once they've got it. The frilled shark uses its 300 teeth to capture prey. Each tooth has three points that look like needles facing backward. If this shark bites a fish, the fish won't be able to escape.

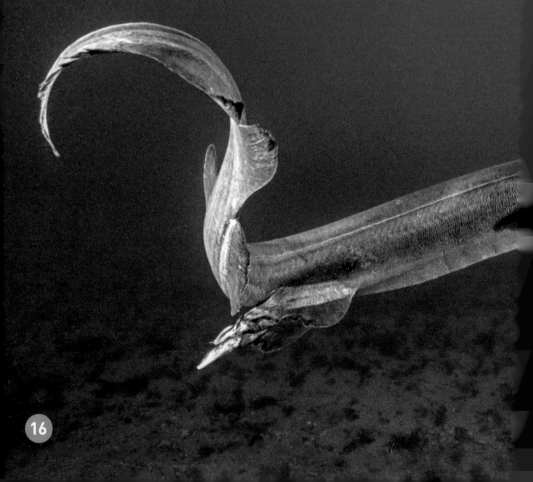

The frilled shark has rows of sharp, pointed teeth that easily grab and hold on to soft prey.

Frilled sharks are called "living fossils" because they have been around for 80 million years.

Atlantic wolffish have sharp fangs to grab prey. They also have three rows of powerful chompers to crush shellfish. Their hardworking teeth wear down and fall out once a year—then they grow a new set!

Wolffish even have teeth in their throats!

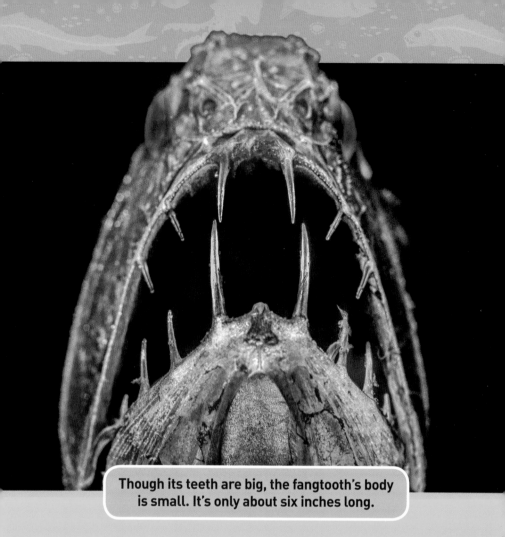

Though its teeth are big, the fangtooth's body is small. It's only about six inches long.

The fangtooth has the biggest teeth for its size of any fish in the ocean. Its teeth are so big, its mouth can't close completely.

Since the fangtooth can't see well, it finds food by bumping into its prey. Then it sucks the prey into its mouth and clamps down tight.

Staying Safe

With so many powerful predators in the deep sea, some animals here also need special ways to defend themselves.

One type of sea cucumber, called a sea pig, can throw up its intestines when it feels threatened. This will confuse and scare a predator, causing it to swim away. But don't worry—the sea pig can grow new intestines.

Weird but true!

The sea pig has legs on the top and bottom of its body!

This sea cucumber is sometimes called the "headless chicken monster."

Another type of sea cucumber can "slime" a predator, if it gets bumped hard enough. The predator is so surprised, the sea cucumber has time to escape. The slime also leaves a glowing cloud on the predator. That warns other prey to stay away.

Hagfish also slime their predators, but it's more than just a warning. When a predator bites a hagfish, the hagfish makes slime. The slime swells when it mixes with seawater. It fills the predator's mouth and gills, making the animal choke. Then the hagfish can slip away.

Hagfish can make buckets of thick slime within minutes.

23

This giant isopod (EYE-soh-pod) rolls into a ball when attacked. Then its tough shell protects its soft belly. This defense works so well that many predators don't bother an isopod at all.

Giant isopods are meat-eaters. They mostly eat the bodies of animals that have fallen to the seafloor.

Giant isopods can grow to more than 14 inches long.

Deep-sea animals, like the isopod, often grow bigger than some land animals. Scientists aren't sure why. A similar land animal, the pill bug, is only about a half-inch long. Yet a giant isopod can grow to be about as long as a house cat.

weird but true!

These creatures are so loved in Japan that people have phone cases shaped like giant isopods!

6 COOL FACTS
About Ocean Exploration

In 1964, the *Alvin* was the first vehicle to take humans to the deep sea. Since then, it's helped people make many discoveries, including hundreds of new sea creatures.

1

Scientists can study deep-sea animals by using traps, called landers. Landers have bait (seen here) and motion-activated cameras. They can film animals and bring small samples to the surface.

2

Underwater drones are small remote-controlled vehicles with cameras. They film areas in the deep, dark sea where humans can't go.

3

4 The Five Deeps Expedition, which started in 2018, is exploring the deepest parts of the ocean to find new species and map the seafloor.

Grapefruit-size robots, called miniature autonomous underwater explorers (M-AUEs), give a 3D view underwater. They also help track movements of tiny deep-sea animals called plankton.

5

The ExoSuit is like a space suit for the ocean. It helps humans fight extreme ocean pressure to study things like how deep-sea animals make light.

6

Hidden Away

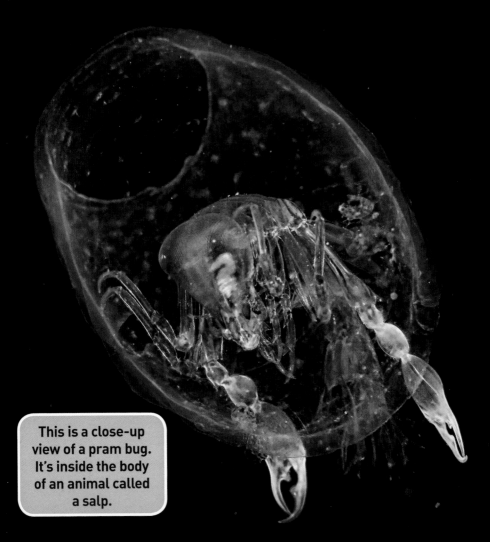

This is a close-up view of a pram bug. It's inside the body of an animal called a salp.

The pram bug is so creepy that people say it inspired sci-fi movie monsters.

The deep ocean floor is pretty empty. There aren't many places to hide when a predator comes your way. So, many animals here have camouflage (KAM-uh-flahj) that hides them from danger.

The pram bug uses its victims as camouflage. Using its sharp claws, the pram bug cuts open prey and eats it from the inside out. Then the tiny creature hides its eggs inside the prey's body. This keeps the eggs safe.

This pram bug and its eggs are protected inside the salp.

Water Word

CAMOUFLAGE: An animal's natural color or form that helps it blend in with what is around it

29

Some creatures have transparent bodies that provide camouflage. This cockatoo squid is sometimes called a "glass squid." Humans can see the patches of red light on its body. But many Midnight Zone animals are not able to see the color red. So it looks invisible.

This is what the cockatoo squid looks like to most animals in the Midnight Zone. Its red patches aren't visible.

Water Word

TRANSPARENT:
See-through, or clear

Sea sapphires shimmer with color for only a few seconds at a time.

The sea sapphire is also transparent—but it sparkles with bright colors. Scientists think this may signal other sea sapphires. Shiny plates on the males reflect light made by other animals. The other animals see a flash of color, then the sea sapphire seems to disappear!

Eyes of the Deep

Many deep-sea animals have special eyes to make use of every bit of light in their deep, dark home.

Mantis shrimp have compound eyes with thousands of little parts that can each see light. These parts work together to spot food and avoid predators. Mantis shrimp can see 12 to 16 different types of light. Humans can only see three.

Water Word

COMPOUND EYES: Eyes that are made up of many smaller parts working together

It looks as if the spookfish has four eyes, but there are only two. The top and bottom parts of each eye are connected.

The brownsnout spookfish's eyes are divided into two parts. One part looks up to spot the shadows of predators and prey. The other part looks down to find tiny flashes of light from other animals. Using a special curved mirror in its eyes, the fish can look above and below it at the same time!

Vampire squid have the largest eyes in the animal kingdom for their body size. Their eyes capture light to spot bits of food called marine (muh-REEN) snow.

Water Word

MARINE SNOW: A mix of tiny creatures, animal remains, and animal poop that floats down to the bottom of the ocean

The telescope octopus has eyes on long tubes that stick out of its head, unlike other octopuses.

Each eye can rotate in a different direction from the other. This helps the octopus see all around it. It swims on its back facing up to avoid predators and to find prey.

The telescope octopus is mostly transparent. Predators can only see its stomach and eyes.

Underwater Party Animals

In deep waters, animals mostly live alone. But scientists found areas where many different types of animals live together in groups. It looks like a party! These animals live near hydrothermal (HI-dro-THUR-mul) vents. Here, the water is warmer and there's more food to eat.

Near the vents, yeti crabs "farm" their own food. Bacteria get trapped and grow in the long hair on the crab's chest and arms. The crab uses its mouth to rake up the bacteria and eat them.

This yeti crab was found in the Dragon Vent in the Indian Ocean.

Giant tube worms live in groups around the vents and grow to be taller than a basketball player. The tube worms don't have mouths, but they don't need them. A type of bacteria lives inside the worms. The bacteria take the chemicals from the vents and change them into food for the tube worms.

Hottest of Homes

Eyeless shrimp live inside the hydrothermal vents, where temperatures can rise above 700 degrees! Because these shrimp can live in such harsh conditions, scientists think they might help us learn about life on other planets.

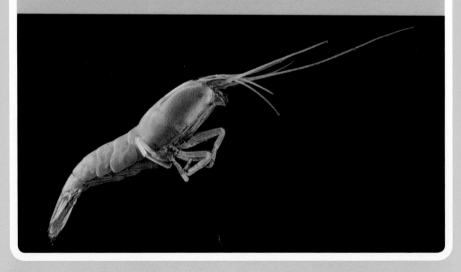

Giant tube worms can grow to be eight feet tall.

A Lot More to Explore!

Scientists have discovered a lot of unusual and alien-looking animals that live underwater. But humans haven't explored 95 percent of Earth's ocean yet. With new technology, who knows what we might discover next?

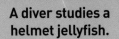

A diver studies a helmet jellyfish.

People in a mini-submarine view a giant barrel sponge on a coral reef near Curaçao.

QUIZ WHIZ

How much do you know about alien ocean animals? After reading this book, probably a lot! Take this quiz and find out.
Answers are at the bottom of page 45.

1

Where in the Midnight Zone do animals live in groups?

A. seaweeds
B. beaches
C. hydrothermal vents
D. shores

2

What does the Midnight Zone NOT have?

A. high pressure
B. strange-looking animals
C. low temperature
D. some sunlight

Which animal can throw up its intestines to confuse predators?

3

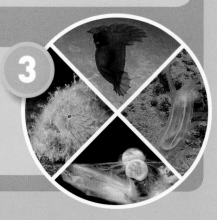

A. headless chicken monster
B. sea pig
C. brownsnout spookfish
D. hairy frogfish

4

Yeti crabs eat _____.

A. marine snow
B. bacteria
C. small fish
D. seaweed

Which animal has the biggest teeth for its size of any animal in the ocean?

A. Atlantic wolffish
B. hairy frogfish
C. frilled shark
D. fangtooth

5

6

What is the name of the first vehicle to take humans to the floor of the deep sea?

A. *Alvin*
B. *Explorer*
C. *Captain*
D. *Alien*

How much of the underwater world is left to explore?

A. 95 percent
B. 85 percent
C. 75 percent
D. 65 percent

7

Glossary

ADAPTATION: A behavior or physical trait that helps a living thing survive in its environment

COMPOUND EYES: Eyes that are made up of many smaller parts working together

HABITAT: A place where animals or plants naturally live

PREDATOR: An animal that hunts and eats other animals

PRESSURE: The force pushing on something

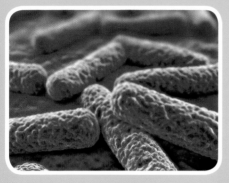

BACTERIA: Certain types of tiny living things that are so small we need a microscope to see them

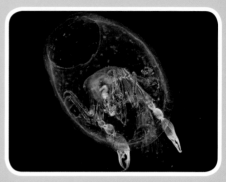

CAMOUFLAGE: An animal's natural color or form that helps it blend in with what is around it

HYDROTHERMAL VENTS: Openings in the ocean floor that release warm water and minerals

MARINE SNOW: A mix of tiny creatures, animal remains, and animal poop that floats down to the bottom of the ocean

PREY: An animal that is eaten by another animal

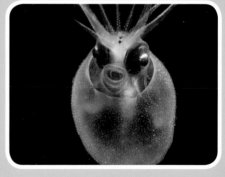

TRANSPARENT: See-through, or clear

Index

Boldface indicates illustrations.

A

Adaptations 14, 15
Alvin (submersible) 26, **26**, **45**
Atlantic long-arm squid 11, **11**
Atlantic wolffish 18, **18**
Atolla jellyfish **12**, 12–13, **13**

B

Bacteria 39, 40
Blue light 13
Brownsnout spookfish 34, **34**

C

Camouflage 29, 30
Challenger Deep, Pacific Ocean 6, **6**
Cockatoo squid 30, **30**
Compound eyes 32, **32–33**
Cutthroat eels 13, **13**

D

DeepSee (submersible) **5**
Drones, underwater 26, **26**

E

E-jellies (electronic jellyfish) 13, **13**
ExoSuit 27, **27**
Eyeless shrimp 40, **40**

F

Fangtooths 19, **19**, **45**
Five Deeps Expedition 27, **27**
Frilled sharks 16–17, **16–17**

G

Giant barrel sponges **43**
Giant isopods **24**, 24–25, **25**
Giant tube worms 40, **41**

H

Hagfish 23, **23**
Hairy frogfish **14**, 14–15, **15**
"Headless chicken monsters" (sea cucumbers) **22**
Helmet jellyfish **42**
Hydrothermal vents **38**, 38–40

J

Jellyfish 11, **12**, 12–13, **13**, **42**

L

Landers (traps) 26, **26**

M

Mantis shrimp 32, **32–33**
Marine snow 35, **35**
Midnight Zone 6, **6**, 7, 8, 14, 16, 30, 40
Miniature autonomous underwater explorers
    (M-AUEs) 27, **27**

O

Ocean
    exploration **4–5**, **26**, 26–27, **27**, 42
    pressure 7, 27
    sunlight 6, 8
    zones 6, **6**

P

Pram bugs **28**, 28–29, **29**

R

Red light 10, 30
Reef fish **15**
Robots, underwater 27, **27**

S

Salps **28**, **29**
Sea cucumbers **20–21**, 21–22, **22**
Sea pigs **20–21**, 21, **44**
Sea sapphires 31, **31**
Slime 22–23
Smalltooth dragonfish 10, **10**
Sunlight Zone 6, **6**

T

Telescope octopuses 36–37, **36–37**
Twilight Zone 6, **6**

V

Vampire squid 35, **35**
Viperfish **8–9**, 9

Y

Yeti crabs 39, **39**